Mel Bay Presents

CLASSICAL PERIOD MUSIC FOR SAXOPHONE

arranged by J. Michael Leonard

FREE Saxophone Solo download available online!
Visit: www.melbay.com/96530

Visit us on the Web at www.melbay.com — E-mail us at email@melbay.com

Contents

RONDO IN G
WoO 41

Ludwig Van Beethoven
(1770–1827)

Arrangement © 1998 by Mel Bay Publications, Inc. Pacific, Missouri 63069.
All Rights Reserved. International Copyright Secured. BMI.

86
91
94
98

122
125
p
p
129
f
f
133
decresc.
decresc.

MARCHE RELIGIEUSE
From The Opera 'Alceste'

Christoph Von Gluck
(1714–1787)

14

Ossia
8va basso
17
p
p
p
22
dolce
dolce
27
32
mf
p
mf
p

CARO MIO BEN
Cavatina

Giuseppe Giordani
(1743–1798)

19
a tempo
p
mf
cresc.
sf rall.
f
mp
3
G.P.
a tempo
p
mf
cresc.
sf rall.
f
p
23
cresc.
cresc.
27
rall.
poco f
f
tr.
rall.
poco f
f
p
31
a tempo
a tempo
f
p
f

SICILIENNE

Maria Theresia Von Paradis
(1759–1824)

GAVOTTE
From The Opera 'Rosine'

François Joseph Gossec
(1734–1829)

17
mf
p
21
p
pp
25 Più mosso
mf
mp
29
Da capo al Fine
Da capo al Fine

HUNGARIAN RONDO

From "Trio Sonata No. 2, Hob XV/25"

Franz Joseph Haydn
(1732–1809)

Arrangement © 1998 by Mel Bay Publications, Inc. Pacific, Missouri 63069.
All Rights Reserved. International Copyright Secured. BMI.

59
64
69
74
f
f
f
f
cresc.
cresc.
ff
ff

TURKISH MARCH
from "Piano Sonata in A, K.331"

Wolfgang Amadeus Mozart
(1756–1791)

17
cresc.
f
p
p
cresc.
f
p
22
Fine
f
Fine
f
sempre staccato
sf
sf
27
sf
sf
sf
sf
sf
sf
33
p
p
p

37
42
47
52
p
p
mf
mf
p
p
mf
mf
D.C. al Fine
D.C. al Fine
28

ENTR'ACTE TO "ROSAMUNDE"
Op. 26

Franz Schubert
(1797–1828)

21
cresc.
f
p
cresc.
f
pp
27
fp
fp
tr
1.
2.
33
p dolce con espress.
pp sempre staccato
40
p

69
p dolce
pp
75
81
f
mf
87
cresc.
cresc.
f
f
p
pp

MARCH

Carl Maria von Weber
(1786–1826)

Arrangement © 1998 by Mel Bay Publications, Inc. Pacific, Missouri 63069.
All Rights Reserved. International Copyright Secured. BMI.

36

12
cresc.
cresc.
15
pp
pp
20
23
37

AVE MARIA

Luigi Cherubini
(1760–1842)

18
23
mf
27
mp
32
8va (ossia)
cresc.
cresc.

37
8va
f
mf
41
8va
p dolce
pp
47
8va
cresc.
f
p
cresc.
f
pp
52
8va
tr
tr
f

MINUET
from "String Quintet No. 11"

44

27
31
36
40
p
p
p
p
p
ten.
D.C. al Fine
D.C. al Fine

Printed in Dunstable, United Kingdom